# CONSTRUCTING A WITCH

**Helen Ivory** is a poet and visual artist. She edits the webzine *Ink Sweat and Tears*, and teaches for UEA/National Centre for Writing Academy online. She has published six collections with Bloodaxe Books: *The Double Life of Clocks* (2002), *The Dog in the Sky* (2006), *The Breakfast Machine* (2010), *Waiting for Bluebeard* (2013), *The Anatomical Venus* (2019), and *Constructing a Witch* (2024), a Poetry Book Society Recommendation *Fool's World*, a collaborative Tarot with artist Tom de Freston (Gatehouse Press), won the 2016 Saboteur Best Collaborative Work award. A book of collage/mixed media poems, *Hear What the Moon Told Me*, was published by KFS in 2017; a chapbook, *Maps of the Abandoned City*, by SurVision in 2019; and *Wunderkammer: New and Selected Poems* was published by MadHat in the US in 2023.

*The Anatomical Venus* was shortlisted for the poetry category of the East Anglian Book Awards 2019. The cover of *The Anatomical Venus*, which features Helen Ivory's own artwork, won the East Anglian Writers Book by the Cover Award (East Anglian Book Awards 2019). In 2024 she received a Cholmondeley Award from the Society of Authors, an award recognising the achievement and distinction of individual poets.

Her work has been translated into Ukrainian, Polish, Spanish, Croatian and Greek for Versopolis. In November 2023, one of her poems was selected for Poems on the Underground. She has received an Eric Gregory Award from the Society of Authors and was awarded a Developing Your Creative Practice Award from the Arts Council of England to research and write this book which is a direct development from *The Anatomical Venus*. She lives in Norwich with her husband, the poet Martin Figura.

Her website is www.helenivory.co.uk

# HELEN IVORY

# CONSTRUCTING
# A WITCH

BLOODAXE BOOKS

ISBN:  978 1 78037 719 3

First published 2024 by
Bloodaxe Books Ltd,
Eastburn,
South Park,
Hexham,
Northumberland NE46 1BS


www.bloodaxebooks.com
For further information about Bloodaxe titles
please visit our website and join our mailing list
or write to the above address for a catalogue.

Supported using public funding by
**ARTS COUNCIL
ENGLAND**

Cover design: Neil Astley & Pamela Robertson-Pearce.
Cover art: Helen Ivory & Martin Figura


Printed in Great Britain by Bell & Bain Limited, Glasgow, Scotland, on
acid-free paper sourced from mills with FSC chain of custody certification.

drive your iron tongue into my mouth
        fell me of my speaking
                ride me through the streets       dumb beast
     this carnival            of spitting, pissing
  you think it makes a manful man of you?

HELEN IVORY: 'Scold's Bridle'
*The Anatomical Venus*
(Bloodaxe Books, 2019)

# CONTENTS

By the slant of her tone,

you will see the narrator

cuts desire lines with a scalpel.

Turn back now if you fear the devil

is at play on the cutting mat —

guiding her hand, trickling words in her ear.

For, oh she is the weaker vessel;

the devil's gateway to your thirsty hothouse.

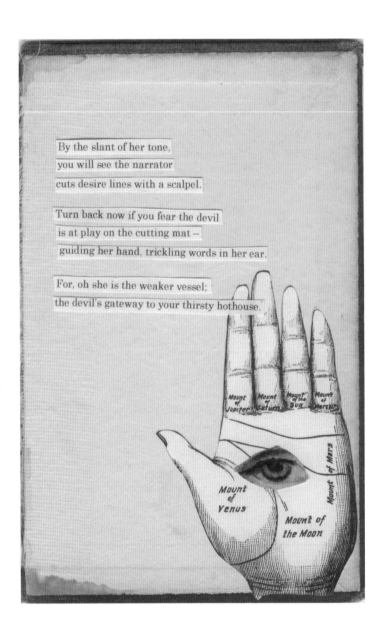

# The Waking

I have become one of those women who goes about with a rattan carriage, salvaging women buried at crossroads or planted out in the woods. One of those women who reconstructs bodies, replacing ligaments with wire. The kind who mixes her own blood with the earth to bring swell to their bones. The kind of woman who tarries with the devil in the naughty light of day – why must we be occult? I hold up those rekindled women and we reel, we howl, and we shoot our filthy mouths off

# Some definitions of *Witch*

Carcass of rags
the dead-rat stink of old milk.
A beyond the pale beggar,
runt of the litter.

\*

Gleaner of herbs
hallower of the compass.
Cunning hedge rider,
measurer of fire.

\*

Midwife of shadows
low vixen with blood on its maw.
Deliverer of silence
to the henhouse.

\*

Lighter than a bible,
priestly ink is gravity
beneath her flying feet.
Her body writes into the sky.

\*

Blended with the earth
she wears a moss cloak.
Some procure her remedies.
She is a scapegoat for bad luck.

*

A childless wraith
in a child's picture book.
The worst mother
man ever invented.

*

The method of kettling
troublesome women.
A peck of black pepper
in the milk-and-water blether.

*

Practitioner of forgotten ways;
of rituals, sayer of spells.
Barefoot earth-listener,
older than God or television.

*The lust of the goat is the bounty of God*

WILLIAM BLAKE: *Proverbs of Hell*


When man made the Devil
he was all strung up on polarities.
Who can we blame for our squalid little sins;
who can take the rap for our immoral bodies?

Man said that God said
put the goats to my left.
Sinister critters; all eyes,
all musk, all appetites.

He drew rough imaginings
of the horned one cavorting with womenfolk
while one might propound, straining hard
against the fabric of his breeches.

*Thus men forgot that All deities reside*
*in the human breast*

    WILLIAM BLAKE: *The Marriage of Heaven and Hell*


Before the first story
sky and the trees sang of themselves
and the seas embraced fishes
as their very own children.
And creatures did as they wont,
not for reasons of story,
but the whyfor of spirit.

When Man uncreatured himself
he made all of the gods
in his selfsame image
and hoisted them up to the sky.
You'll know the stories by now
of the smiting of gods
till just the King of all Kings remained.

You'll know too, it hardly needs saying
that Man said that God said
Man needed a helpmeet
a soft-fleshed companion –
the garden was a lonely place, after all.
So in God's name he created a Woman
to take in his laundry.

What happens then is written in pictures –
she, clothed entire in a snake
she, tearing fruit with her teeth
she, charming him join her in all the tree's knowledge;
the bite of flesh that sticks in his craw.
This was the first test and they failed,
though it was decreed that she failed it more.

17

*Wouldst thou like to live deliciously?*

BLACK PHILLIP: *The VVitch*, 2015


I have marked you
at the gateway to the forest
inhaling the wildwood like medicine.

And I have sent the most velvet of hares
as a gift of my heart
to usher you from the burdensome world.

You have been the pious daughter –
washed your father's rags in the brook.
Have you not earnt enough of god's grace?

Your parents bade you pray for light
while heaping shadows round your character.
Harken as they brand you *witch*, without a lick of proof.

Come follow, I have such bounty for you.
There is always a little bloodshed
when a woman is born.

## Another Story

I was skirring around
as a drift of quarks and electrons –
I was barely an I, let me explain.

I was called into being by some god, I believe,
as it stood on a mountain
in high strappy boots
and frantically appealed
for *a beast to minister the wretched.*
Ousting is simpler than caring, I suppose.

The door was held open, so I trotted in.
Once my horned head was in place
I screwed it on tight
and looked around me for someone to love.

They say I *had use of* the widow
but that's not how I saw it
and neither did she when the kittling was born
and brought light to her desolate house.

Now think on that, goodly bodies
when you toss your spilled salt in my eye
or nail an iron horseshoe to your door.

## We are the weirdos, mister

NANCY DOWNS: *The Craft*, 1996

A skyful of rain meddles in
through a rubble of rooftiles.
Serpents unleash in all their forms
and the girls themselves
are every manner of weaponless
in their damaged, orphan skins.

Let's not focus on how it all turns out
but on the necessity of the coven;
of pulling on an armour of black velvet
and drinking of your sister's blood,
elixir in a cup of wine called Ariel,
the angel of *earth, fire, water, air.*

Each lit candle is a breath of light in the pitch
oh, the urgency of chanting:
       *now is the time, now is the hour*
       *ours is the magic, ours is the power,*
and twenty-seven years later
anonymous, on YouTube's wall:
       *I wouldn't be here without my sisters*

daughters of air

look through the glass

Seest thou not how strong she is?

# The Answer

It was a wonder no one noticed when they cut the woman in half. Not from side to side, as they do in workaday cabaret acts, but straight down the middle. A perfect bisection. Making use of the smoke and mirrors left behind by the illusionist, she appeared, both of her, to walk away on two legs to two different locations.

One went home to her family and scrubbed down the hearthstones. The other stole deep into the woods and was presently joined by a cat with a murderous yowl.

When her stepchildren arrived quarrelsome, too late for dinner, stomping their muddy hoofs all through the house, she sent them out to the woods. Let her deal with them there, she thought. She stood in front of the mirror, smiling as crookedly as a good woman is able.

## Only Bad Witches Are Ugly

GLINDA THE GOOD: *The Wizard of Oz*, 1939

Do you light from the skies in the blush of a bubble
your gown all glamoured with stars,
or does the earth spew you forth in a retch of red smoke?

Are you more peaches and cream or frog in a quagmire;
opiate stoned in a cradle of poppies
or rattled awake in the dash of a blizzard?

Are you gooder than good in a basket of good
unbinding the bad with your charming white wand,
or is your scandalous body the root of your power?

*Are you a good witch, or are you a bad witch?*

# The Woman of Endor to Saul

Do not turn to mediums or necromancers;
do not seek them out, and so make yourselves unclean by them:
I am the Lord your God.

LEVITICUS 19:31


How predictable that you should come to me
now your unworldly god has turned his face away.
Your dreams won't help; your messengers
have stopped their ears and tied their tongues –
you may as well go supplicate a field of weeds.

It's understandable your manners fail you now
your glory lies about your feet,
your kingdom thrown so heedlessly away.
My weakness is I can't shut out a desperate soul –
I am a human woman, though they brand me *witch*.

When I bring up Samuel from the dead
I'll make myself a veil between the worlds.
This is natural, light of spirit – no dark art or seduction
and Samuel's words will be his words
even if they're not the words you want to hear.

You must agree to this before I summon him –
I do not undertake this without peril to myself.

# Night Hag

It begins with a nightmare that rides you deep into the forest's yawn. And the forest at first is all heart with its mothering arms and plentiful kindling. Soon enough the trees will fall barren and their branches claw through the skin of your sleep. When you wake gasping, she climbs from your chest, complexion the tincture of liverwort. The vial in her clasp holds your stolen breath and your body is dead as can be.

# One Such Tale

After a vast night of walking,
the shadow happened upon the tor
and arranged herself nicely
among the high-grazing sheep.

She knew she wasn't a sheep
but the sheep did not craze –
none lifted their heads
from the sky sweet grass.

She yearned in her heart to be given a name
to be called for, to have bearings
so when the shepherd appeared
the shadow cleared her throat.

*What am I?* She implored, in a voice
she thought kind as a rockpool.
Oh, but the shepherd was sapling of spirit
and he ran and he ran, screaming pestilence

and thence flew about the village
recounting a starless fairy
that turned his blood to winter
and ripped at his manhood with her claws.

## Scry

Let's put a crow in this box. Let's push the dead of night to the corners of this cage and harken what it has to say. With its clicks and its rattles and its shimmering black. With its iniquitous weather and beak full of blood. What oblivion will it wreak here? Which Fury will it bring? Draw in close now. Soft-focus on the black mirror of its eye.

# Day's Conversation with Night

The sun was glory on the tip of my tongue
and every creeping thing and flying thing
cast the rays of its eyes all about. Do you remember?
Nothing was occult, lambs cut capers
and no brute's maw closed on any throat.
Life was lustre, unbruised fruit
till you dragged your dogs across the sky
and in your wake, a plaguey mess.

*The Dark wrapped the earth in ragged clouds*
*and began to croon a death song for Day –*
*summoning it to its own remembering:*

When you were a cub, on that first day
you invented a theatre of charcoaled timbers
and drew back the curtains, quiet as an owl.
The lanterns cast a low wash of blue
and your imagination stalked in from the wings.
Do you recall how those long winter nights
felt in your hands as you knitted them
into a pall you named *Dark* from your seat in the gods?

Monsters – some slithered, some crept from my folds
in a bristling derangement of nature
while downstage beldams held to a seething crucible
their faces awake with a terrible light.
I am thunderstruck you cannot summon this.
How you painted fear so vividly inside the heads of men!
Day, you have clammed up since that early grandiosity.
I've grown too old to close the curtains on this all.

## More thoughts about the dark

If you take the dark for a walk across the ordinary light of this page it will cover its eyes. It will grovel down inside its fur and beg to be taken to a time before language. The dark elects for inchoate echoes, where the imagination scratches pictures inside the hippocampus with its imaginary claw. The dark is not a nice man. The dark strenuously objects to honey owing to its close connection with the sun. When you open your mouth you pour into the dark. When the dark opens its mouth it pours into you. Have a care for the dark.

# The Antihousewife

The witch is an antihousewife

DIANE PURKISS: *The Witch in History*, 2013

It must have been the cow bewitched –
some slippage of verse in the maid's lullaby
that tainted the milk beyond fleeting.

Or the spinster's words as she passed your door
that whipped up the flames to a vigorous lick
so the milk did not seethe, only scald and reek.

O how slyly stranger milk finds egress;
how it skims off the tongue, slicks down the throat.
A goodwife must guard her family's inattentive supping.

# Dairying

And suddenly the devil takes the milk from the udder of
that cow, and brings it to where the witch is sitting, as if it
were flowing from the knife.

REVS KRAMER AND SPRENGER: *Malleus Maleficarum*, 1486

Rue this shift from grass
to seething, blood dashed mess
in the pregnant bellied
boiling pot
where milk roils
its blighted self about,
making of the hearth
a corrupt place.

Come smithy
with your scalding iron,
unwitch this noise!
Come purify
come cauterise
come still with righteous fire
this breathing,
she-made grief.

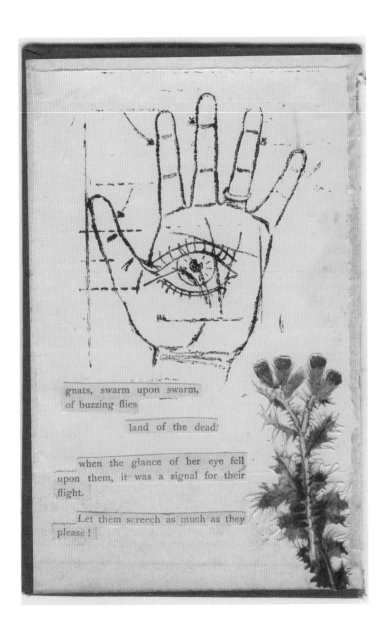

gnats, swarm upon swarm,
of buzzing flies

land of the dead.

when the glance of her eye fell
upon them, it was a signal for their
flight.

Let them screech as much as they
please!

# Remedy

When down the steeply hill misfortune comes like stones upon your head; when putrefaction spreads among your crops, convulsions dance your daughter to her grave and you can see no godly reason, nor end to havoc, what else is there to do? With your grief and threadbare wits, you seek the wisdom of the pellar.

She tells you that to break the spell to search your pantry for a stoppered bottle. Add rose thorns, rusted pins and a half moon of your fingernail. Douse with wine, your urine, equal measure, so to drown the witch, snagged upon those foraged barbs on her journey from the otherworld.

Bury this receptacle intact, sealed with wax, in the furthest corner of your house. Thus, the necromancy be reversed and the witch's human shape, purged forever from this world. Amen.

# How to Construct an Ale Witch

She is a tonnysh gyb;
The devyll and she be syb.

JOHN SKELTON: *The Tunning of Elenor Rumming*, 1545

Assemble the materials
to fabricate a crooked alewife hat;
spring scissors, wire, dark cloth.
Build it high enough
to spot her in the marketplace.
Why make it difficult, Gentlemen?

Now rootle out the mouser
that stalks her barley store.
Harken how she calls to it
in that unchristian tongue?
Overturn the cauldron
and let her midden burn.

She is the very screech owl
that hunts inside the rookery heads
of all the King's fine men.
Prepare yourself a godly brew
free of rabbit scut and bad magic;
build your factories, count your coins.

# New Rules for the Disenchanted Land

> The human body and not the steam engine,
> and not even the clock, was the first machine
> developed by capitalism
>
> SILVIA FEDERICI: *Caliban and the Witch*

Cleanse yourself of incantations,
those superstitious acts employed
when taking beasts into the field –
you cannot sing grass sweet.

Nor can you cajole the rain to fall
or placate some green spirit of the fields
to augment propagation.
You have no power but in your arms.

It is understood that hags exist
who'll feast upon a suckling's flesh.
There are occult doings in alleyways –
mixed potions of wild wormwood and such.

Trust not your women with their bodies –
the unproductive womb is a sin
and furthermore, a hindrance to progress:
we need more small hands to scare away the crows.

# Cackle

A golden padlock I wear on my mouth at all times so that
no villainous words shall escape from my mouth

ANTON WOESNAM: *The Wise Woman*, c. 1525

The women are at it again;
gossiping at the childbed
where the gateway to all malevolence itself
is a folly tale away.

And the soul of that poor mite,
still streaked in birth blood
and unreceived by God –
such carelessness, such sloppy mouths.

Now hear the washers at the river
loose-hair, bare-breasted,
swapping tips, tongue to tongue
of how to be a spiteful scold.

They feed the devils
scratching at their parchments
with all that filthy prattle;
with all that rattles base in this world.

And so, you forge a branks
to gash the voices from their maws.
You choke them till they learn to say
I love you in a pretty way.

NOTE: Etymology. The word 'gossip' is from Old English *godsibb*, from
*god* and *sibb*, the term for the godparents of one's child or the parents of
one's godchild, generally very close friends. From the 16th century the
word has come to mean a person (mostly a woman) who delights in idle
talk, rumours and tattling.

# The Gift

There once was a lonely woman who replaced her heart with an apple. She took a sharp knife and engraved her name in its freshly shined skin, and those of the names of these spirits: *Cosmer, Synady, Heupide*. She stood in the middle of a bridge as the wind heaped bright dying leaves all about. She balanced the apple in the palm of her hand, but nobody came for her love. And the earth moved through the seasons, and still nobody came. This carried on till the apple resembled some devil they say, and the woman herself had transmuted to dust.

One day a quiet pandemonium emanated from the apple and the townspeople hid behind themselves, too cowed to approach. A man stepped from the crowd with the air of a judge. He decreed that indeed, the apple was infested with foul spirits, and pitched it into the river with his long-legged boot.

# Fetish to Counteract Witchcraft

It is supposed that hearts of beasts
are infused with the spirits of their prey;
that breath breathed upon their prey
and back into the heart
is charged with powerful magic.

That such beasts overwhelm their quarry
demonstrates their sovereignty.
There is further evidence these powers are preserved
when the heart is cut from the body
and the body putrefies into the ground.

If witchcraft is suspected in your flock,
if it is seized by foot-rot, the fluke or bottle-jaw
and sheep are dying in the fields,
fiercely stick the heart with thorns and nails
while fixating on the malady astir.

Thus, the attendant witch will be revealed.
Watch close for any lowly hag
evincing untoward disorders.
Act swift now, like a bird of Jove
closing down its prey.

and thus the riddle has been read. Homeward!
homeward!

# The Moon's Halo

Rain has been quarrelsome the whole night long and raps at the door to come in. Rain is the sky's voice, the moon's halo. Rain is bedlam on the stone body of the house – spiders have forsaken their meticulous webs. Rain is the marriage of toads. A tatty jackdaw cleaves to ridge tiles combing weather from its wings. You invert a pan in the yard to appeal to rain's kinder nature. In some kitchen a shadow ties nine knots in a bight of frayed string, for this cat-and-dog flood. Step out in rain on the day of a funeral and god's tears will drown you the rest of your life.

## Protection Ink

Do not think by these printed words I make myself vulnerable
to the clocks that walk about the place with graveyard dirt
on their boots, tut-tutting disingenuously about the waste of
it all. The ink I use is dragon's blood with oil of cinnamon.
To be plainer still, I do not speak of the stylings set on the
page you are reading. The true words are drawn in an
unbroken circle with me at the pivot. Here all my shadows
are cleaved to the walls. And no clock can reach in with its
meddling hands and bucket of caustic to scour me away.

# At the Witchcraft Museum

Folk tarry round the poppets,
those pin-jabbed wax unfortunates –
receptacles for ill-wishing
who've carried grief inside
their tallow bodies
for perhaps a hundred years.

And the heart-pierced doll
whose every knitted stitch is taut
with a focussed hate – each casting on,
each incision and every tensioned yarn
repeats the curse, repeats the curse
to bind it, fix it, make it so.

Some chuckle at the recent ones, shop bought,
Trump-themed, complete with pins and guidance
on how to make his hair fall out
or strike bigotry from his tongue.
If this fails to make a mark, it says –
reverse over him with your car.

On the web you can procure a felt Putin –
you're urged to *stick it to him*
*like he has stuck it to the world.* 449 sales so far.
He's hand-sewn; his face a photograph.
*Three people have this in their baskets right now.*
This item is described as *a parody*.

# Hexentanz

But, after all, isn't a bit of witch hidden
in every female?

MARY WIGMAN, dancer, 1926

Not the new-fangled Witch Dance
throwing shapes over TikTok,
this is frank choreography
cast out its line to pronounce a web
on the burnished sprung floor of *Suspiria*.

To be inside language – the body as prayer,
as incantation, a strike of lightning.
To be earthed and barefoot
to be creature; muscle and cells.
To fly; to know space beneath you.

And who needs music when you have breath,
when you are daughter to the Mother of Sighs?
Put on your rope dress of red human hair.
Paint out your mouth with a broad white stroke.
We are the palace of wands, sticky with silk.
We send you our dreams, little wren, undone.

# Häxan

O holy mother, the evil one has terrible power!

BENJAMIN CHRISTENSEN: *Häxan*, 1921

Midnight, dark as a cellar,
the auteur casts himself as Devil
all twisty-horned, all snake-tongue flicker,
all frantic mortar, grinding hard into pestle
at threshold after beckoning threshold.

Sister Cecilia's eyes, wide as twin mouths
as she connives with himself
for ah she is hungry for dancing,
for laughing fierce till she's tipsy
and lost to herself; to this dolorous world.

Fever sweeps over the convent
till all the sisters reel
with lecherous outthrust tongues,
the heavy fabric of their habits
agitating like an anarchy of bats.

Cut to a fallen sister cradling the carved Son of God.
She spits on his crown, a low baptismal drool –
looks heavenward, beseeches:
*Burn me at the stake pious fathers!*
Her face is an unmarked grave.

44

# The Original Bad Girl

DANTE GABRIEL ROSSETTI: *Lady Lilith*, 1887

We've seen your faces, Lilith
this one sanctioned by the Brotherhood.
It is unimportant you began with one face
yet by the time the paint had dried
you were someone else.

No, not someone else –that's not the point.
You are an *Enchantress*; you don't wear socks
or nip to the shop for a bag of potatoes.
This is your rectangle of pictorial space;
these are your flowers, torpid with symbolism.

That bad girl attitude you sometimes wear
translates here as *narcissism* –
Oh, you love that mirror
and how it takes you in.
Dante can't get a fair shake, poor lamb.

He's done that thing with your hair
so that you're inviting the viewer to feel the tension
as the locks are pulled taut
and one can imagine them springing back
like a fiery trap. Then they're done for.

## To a Painter

How, pray, is your cow skin glue
distinct from charming?
You take the hide and tendons, hooves
boil them up in that scarred cauldron.
And the stench enough to bid the beasts
from many miles, all slaver-mawed –
more quarry for your pot!

Fancy keeps you company
while your bed is bare;
idle hands grope for brushes –
ah! such renderings of midnight!
You are haunted by flesh are you not.
I wonder if this exorcism purifies
or stirs up the appetite?

Paint me now astride a broomstick
my contorted face all seized by flight.
Depending on my time of life
I am the maid ripe for corruption
or the long-dugged ruined hag,
while you sir, are fixed rigid;
the loudest voice, all penn'orth spent.

## All about the hair

Bound for the town square, her hair was worked to squally red by quarrelling air, then to all-devouring fire, and then to snakes of sundry class. Her eyes were mirrors one minute – staring stones, the next. If you looked upon her, you'd have to look away or see yourself entire – or never see another thing on this earth again.

She'd come for babies. To make some, or to round them up for breakfast. Her hair was a rope of multi-function. Many would kill for the shine of it. Perhaps bathing in the untainted blood of babies added to its youthful sheen. It didn't bear thinking about.

# More thoughts about the body

If you take her to the sea she will kick like a fish. When the moon pulls her from her cave, she writes it a postcard with her own blood. She looks nothing like, everything like the paintings that have been made about her. She is mutable as the day is long. If you tie a bell to her ankle, she will stuff it with moss. Lately she has attempted to cast off flesh. She has been observed dropping it off at Lost Property in a neat leather bag. She has been seen on a Greek mountain balancing her head upon the tip of a finger.

a cluster of pretty berries

in the deepest of wells

their colour fadeth, their flesh rotteth.

approach of a tempest

marks of their wickedness.

You are now in the
Cavern of the Winds.

49

# Margaret Johnson

*1633, Pendle Witch Trials*

Days were moonless, drab
and I was a sack of bones
in my widow-house.

Seven years this went –
part-sombre, part-vexed,
wholly disremembering of the sun.

Then he came, all silk-garbed, all sleek furred –
and the promises!
it was as if he'd heard my prayers indeed.

He pricked my flesh
supped my slow blood till I quickened
and felt my spirit siphon into him.

Though I repent this transaction now
I had no prestige until the devil
lodged his shadow at my hearth.

Since this trouble hatched, he has forsaken me.
I cannot send my spirit out
to avenge those who need tormenting.

Yet history casts me out as *not a witch* –
if I was *not* a witch,
how did I meet the night's wings? how did I fly?

# Elizabeth Tibbots

*1672, Stoneleigh*

Time goes, people go;
their names and majesty
all sawdust swept
between flagstones.

Yet you call me
and three centuries dead
I'm up on two legs
in your room.

You might fancy
I walked these years
in the shape of a dog
in quest of an audience.

You've a hankering
to see how I vomit up
a pocket pistol,
a pair of pincers –

you'll want to examine
my throat for signs of violence,
my flesh for claw marks.
I'm here; let us make the most of it.

# Lilias Adie

*(c. 1640-1704)*

Witch who had sex with the Devil

*Daily Mirror*, 2017

And still the clickbait designed to pique a fever –
though clicking arrives you at a neighbourly face
conjured up forensically.

She'd been six foot tall, according to her bones,
buried intertidally, like suicides –
pressed down by a stone to dam reanimation.

Such wickedness requires a belt and braces execution.
Who's to say the devil will not wake her
to bring about more sickness to the fold?

A podcast now, and Lilias' confession, we learn,
is duplication of another peasant woman's admission,
some fifty years before:

*The devil put one hand on the crown of my head*
*another on the soles of my feet*
*and claimed everything between as his.*

Then you learn they lost her skull
a hundred years ago, and the image of her face
is drawn from photographs.

And her bones were gathered up as trinkets –
even wood from her coffin you can see in a museum
whittled to a walking stick, fancied up with silver.

# Walking the Witch

The negative impacts of prolonged sleep deprivation
include psychological, neurological, and physiological effects
that affect many bodily systems

*Psychology Today*, on torture, 2020

i saw a suckling mouth
familiar as my own dead girl
and the devil would restore her
    if i gave him a son

in his lace collar, a gentleman
    tall and dark he flew as a raven
                had use of my body
and night was the underside of a raven's wing

dark-beaked angel
    he spoke out their names
brother and sister of the netherworld
        *Beleth, Hecate come unto me*


in the gaol they watched me        the nights
    they walked me
they watched me      the nights
    they walked me      the days
        they walked me      god spare me
           and this is what i said

# The Devil's Mark

I am naked in the rawest sense.
Clothes, then hair –
even in the most private of places –
ripped sore with a dirty blade.

This is their enquiry,
a science in God's name.
A proof of how Satan raked an owner's claw
across the parchment of my skin.

Nature marked me out, they said
Showed the dark one I was open for trade.
A blood red freckle here,
a stain the cast of a skull, on my behind.

If they cut into my heart
they would find a crucifix inverted
and my faithless womb would harbour a demon.
These were the facts of it.

They say it was the Devil had me
yet I sharp recall the human meat of man
and his beery breath up close.
The Devil wore a poacher's coat.

# More thoughts about the Witch Finder

> There is no doubt that certain witches can do marvellous
> things with regard to male organs, for this agrees with what
> has been seen and heard by many, and with the general
> account...
>
> REVS KRAMER AND SPRENGER: *Malleus Maleficarum*, 1486

He is a human man on a sea of blood. When he closes down
his eyes, he divines undersea caves where there ought to be
mouths in the faces of every woman, but his own mother
and that of the mother of God. He sits tall in the saddle, a
grubby angel at each flank. At the end of a day's grind his
heavy purse plays against his hip like a languorous whore.

Shall the boys come
and hang, burn, or roast you? Wait
a little, I will call them!"

# Pendle Tourist

Some tellings raise the curtain on old Demdike and Chattox
outwitching each other with herbs and with curses
and selling protections to put bread on their tables.

Some fix on Alizon and her suckling black dog;
how she begged pins from a pedlar for tacking a dress,
or a love charm. Either way he refused, and she cursed him.

Soon after he suffered a stroke, they say now.
Though in his eyes, to her mind, she witched him lame
with the aid of the dog who spoke human words.

You come here having read all the books
try to reckon treading these rain-dark hills
without Gore-Tex, or the money in your bank to buy pins.

If a dog stood on two legs in the middle of the track
how much would you give him to conjure you back?
What would you trade for the words to set here?

# Bridget Bishop

*b. 1632 Norwich England d. 1692 Salem, Colony of Massachusetts*


She strides dead through the centre of Witch City
past the statue of Elizabeth Montgomery
with its cute nose and spurious broom;
she strides out in her Paragon Bodice
gaudy as blood on God's laundered sheets.

He sees her, Judge Corwin, that slatternly Eve
titivating her ribbons in the dress shop window.
And all about, uncivilly walking in streets on the Sabbath –
the Eves; uncovered hair, tattooed naked arms.
They ought to be stripped and whipped raw.

Their spectres never meet – that is, she is oblivious of him.
If a candle burns blue, she doesn't see it
so rapt is she in the fire of the living.
He levels his hat against this meddling tempest.
His collar is tight on his neck, these days.


NOTE: Jonathan Corwin was a New England magistrate and one of the
judges involved in the Salem witch trials.

# The Good People of Salem

When the saints claimed Naumkeag, they named it *Peace*. They stole all of the fish in the ocean and wiped out the locals with rifles and microbes. They banned dancing and Christmas and all rags of popery.

The Reverend Parris preached to his shuddering flock of the Dragons of war – the enemy of the righteous – and that the Devil and his instruments were thick in their midst. Witches & Wizards crept among them. They prayed fierce they remained on the side of the good but the door to their lusts was flimsy.

NOTE: Native Americans lived in northeastern Massachusetts for thousands of years prior to European colonisation of the Americas.

Those referred to as Puritan called themselves terms such as 'the godly', 'saints', 'professors', or 'God's children'. They named Salem after the Hebrew word 'shalom', which means 'peace'.

# Samuel Parris Dreams of Dogs

> The Devils prevalency in this Age is most clear in the
> Marvailous number of Witches abounding in all places.
> Now.
>
> SAMUEL PARRIS: Sermon, Salem, 1692

The dogs tied up in the barn are doomsayers of the highest order. They bark at the sea, at the oncoming tides, although they cannot see them with their own very eyes. They hear the approach of occult spirits by cartload after whining cartload. They feel the march of fleas in their coats, little devils, piercing their skin with their mouthparts. The sun creeps over the floor but the dogs are always in shadow. Midnight hangs over their heads like a bone sharp tomahawk.

## The Makings

There were sprits in the fire
shadows stood about,
livestock gone lame, fever
and that perpetual winter
that nearly finished us all.

On those grounds
we festooned a flesh and bones puppet
placed green wood all about –
thence the burning was slow
and we all warmed our hands.

The wails didn't matter
because she was not human
she was barely a *she*;
a barren nothing, a wraith
fused together by spite.

# Witchfinder Tour

*Mistley, Essex*

We bring torches to light our feet. Our guide does not believe
in spirit sightings, frowns on flash photography and has a
shaky grip on history. She stands beside traffic, yells about
drowning and slow strangulation as if she were hawking
potatoes. By way of a séance, she arranges us in an unhallowed
circle beside Old Knobbley, then whinnies her come-hithers
to the rush-hour chill.

NOTE: Old Knobbley is the 800-year-old oak tree growing in woodland in
Mistley, Essex. It is said that the tree was part of the woodland where
those accused of witchcraft might have sought sanctuary.

# Mistley Pond Washes its Hands

Water says it knows nothing
on this sharp December day –
even light can't find a portal
through the algae's green bloom.

Water declares it's *tabula rasa*;
it's a commonplace pond
has merely grown fishes, slaked cattle
these hundreds of years.

You have questions, as does the rook
from its high dying branch.
*Look at the field and the trees* water says,
*how brightly new! I am their like!*

The rook's not distracted
though you look away –
a slim dog whips your attention
to the land's living edge.

Water tries for a sly cough
but belches ugly to the so crisp air,
and quicksmart you're all eyes
with the crackerjack rook.

Now water stands back from itself
chants its formula
with the empiricism of a school master
*two parts hydrogen, one part oxygen...*

The rook can see them – the swum accused
choking death from their lungs –
*two parts hydrogen, one part sulphur*
he rasps, till you see them too.

NOTE: Between 1644 and 1646 Matthew Hopkins, the Witchfinder
General used Mistley Pond for 'swimming', 'ducking' or drowning
alleged witches during the Essex Witch Trials.

familiar spirits

sisters in the twilight

Would you like to fly away free to the woods?

# More thoughts about the moon

Someone picked the moon to be your avatar.
Swooned up on your beauty
he invented the metaphor for the fulgent,
unreachable conundrum of your presence.

When he got a grip on gravity, he blathered on
about the heady dance of earth and moon
in each other's gravitational pull.
He'd set himself up as *the earth*, of course.

His ardour in your maiden and your mother days
was resolute, but as you *waned* (his word)
he could only see the *carrion* (that old word for crone)
scraping dead flesh off the underpass.

A goddess is a goddess is a goddess;
why rename her as she orbits you, oh earth?
And if she appears all *dark of the moon*
it is because your rotation is too fast.

The moon's path around the earth is widening
by the wingspan of a wood nymph moth, each year.
Perhaps it's finally time to take a hint.
It seems she'd rather lay her bets on emptiness.

# Prick

'Witches' and 'Whores': The Far Right Is Already
Celebrating the End of Abortion

VICE.COM, 3 May 2022

If you hold a gun to my head
if you wake and walk me night on night
if you prick my flesh with a bodkin
hunting down the witch's mark
if you crush my bones, skewer my tongue
claw off my breasts with an Iron Spider
if you bind my limbs
and drop me in the deepest lightless inland sea

if you practise all due process
in a court of law
and what remains of my breath is phantom
then, then you can take use of my womb.

Pull your trigger, plant your seed
grow all God's blond and shining children.

# Resistance Spells

*Spell to Take Back the Night*

As a fox, then. A rust blade
through the beer belly of midnight;
that's how it goes.

Take to your workbench
crack the nitrogen bubbles in your knuckles,
gather your fibres and needles.

Do it now, as the sun crosses the street
all hands in its pockets;
all devil-may-care.

The barbs of your needle
stabbed into the fibres
will ravel them in on themselves.

When your hide is complete
and you are fixed safe inside
then you shall go to the ball.

## Summoning Spell: The Body

Call back blood to blood.
Call back the spectacle of flesh.
Fasten on your head with wire,
hold it like a scrying ball
in your savvy hands.

You will see now, clear as clear
the acid burns, the lotus feet,
the force-fed and the skinnied-down.
Your face floats just below
the surface of the glass.

Midwife your very body home
from every shabby playboy den
and launder up the air with smudging sage.
Call back the spectacle of flesh.
Call back blood to blood.

## Disarming Spell: The Enchanter

This is a lesson in forgetting;
unpicking yourself
from the love song he constructed
which you ruined for him
with your clumsy ways.

This is when you stop saying sorry;
when you decide what shoes to wear.
Trace a circle around yourself;
use the wingspan of your arms
to gather all the sky you need.

From this leeway you will behold
the woman who trod warily
about her daily chores;
the one who bit her tongue so much
her words were rendered void.

If you desire it, tromp barefoot –
the critic spitting résumés
on how you have performed each day
has melted clean away.

This is furthermore
a lesson in self-conjuring.

NOTE: The United Nations defines violence against women as: any act of gender-based violence that results in, or is likely to result in, physical, sexual, or mental harm or suffering to women, including threats of such acts, coercion or arbitrary deprivation of liberty, whether occurring in public or in private life.

The church-bells began to ring of their own accord

whereupon she awoke from her trance

# 'Grandmother Moorhead's Aromatic Kitchen'

LEONORA CARRINGTON, 1975


The outside moon lilts from its pulpit
while at the threshold
a shadow nurses a bowl of its light.

Mother Goose closes her eyes
as her daughters invoke her
from a circle described on the scullery floor.

At her shoulder, a patient goat
waits to enter the circle,
a besom upright at her flank.

The blood-painted walls
are charged with the incense of onions,
with peppers, with gnarled heads of garlic

which rise from the page
of this book I've been reading,
transforming my snow-coloured room.

# The Watcher

She walks backwards into the sea;
shingle gives ingress to her feet
before erasing any word of her.

At her shoulder a scrappy halfmoon
of grey seals pause their morning hunt
to study this rum spectacle.

Her cotton shift loses a little pigment
day-by-day, so the dark blooms
are an unreadable cloud below the surface.

From the cliffs, you can see her, if you wish it.
And when the wind drops just enough,
glass armonica seal-song becalms you.

Go to her now, she will send back your dead
and salvage your bedazzling treasures.
She can feel you are heartsore.

# The Happenings

This tree is the spit of the tree you saw when you set out on this crosscut and were drawn into the darkly green heart of the breathing woods. Every tree is the spit of that tree. You scuffle through gorse and a shadowtail shrieks.

At last, a clearing and a glimpse of the goodly sky. How rare it is to see a gentleman's finery about these parts, a man in black – priestlike and orderly. He removes his hat in greeting, and of course you bow as well as you can, in your rabbity way, wishing the forest would gather you up.

\*

The tall shadow followed you, that's what you tell them. How else to account for its voice in the den of your ear. Folk have ceased to call at your door. Your grain store is abandoned, save the bitty stirrings of rats.

Since Samhain your fire will not burn, no scrap of flame. The grain dolly tacked to the lintel does nothing but weep. You tell no one of this; best to keep muzzled. The shadow is louder at night when the birds are at roost. It has taken up residence in your dead father's chair and knows all the old songs so well, it sings them backwards. Sometimes the lace collar round the shadow's neck seems to resemble a horned-moon, fallen to its back.

\*

The priest called today – you spied his dark-clad shape from the goat-shed. It's lovely to hide with the goats, to be coddled in their mother-smell and living heat. By and by he went away, his entourage of rooks *hroc hroc*ing their disappointment.

He'd come about your soul but what good's a soul in this world when no one will buy your ale? At dusk, you watched her fleet through the lane as hare, jinking off into the low meadow. Lately your body is heavy as a sack of grain.

\*

The last time you saw your mother she'd made a hallowed circle by the beck. She was barefoot and cradled at its heart. She'd gone to meet with spirits and her body bided like an empty cup awaiting rain.

\*

All these men in their dainty vestments with their bosky intent – your mother would have had something to say about them. You hear her voice always at the edge of land. You know that if you reached into any hull of water, she would be there to pull you down into safety. But the notion of the between-state frightens you. The spirit leaves the body with such joy, yet the body, dear she suffers, earthly creature full of sorrow.

\*

You spent the winter with the goats. Some days even the sun was so tired it barely opened its eye. You'd decided to leave the shadow to its own tricks and could hear its low croon as it dragged itself to every corner of the house.

\*

By the time spring arrived, the shadow couldn't lift its dim self from the floor. It was songless as a worm. The chimney had forgotten everything it ever knew about fire.

The piebald goat urged you return to the house – to at least peek through the window and get a sense of how things were. Advice from goats was commonly sound, you'd come to believe.

*

The white goat is pregnant and has been grazing the orchard with something close to serenity. You follow the path she has cropped to the house, the piebald at your side.

When you open the latch, there is a sudden scuttling, and all at once, you are a standing stone. The goats move close, remind you that you are a living woman and so you push your shoulder to the door. A tiny patch of night crawls into the sun and dies.

*

The grain dolly has sprouted green where her toes and fingers should be. You clean the grate of ashes and build, from seasoned oak, what seems like the first fire. It needs no coaxing to surge into life and presently the chimney roars out to the sky with the glory of it all.

The goats nibble at the lush clover grown from every surface of the room. You, in the bright garden of your home. You, the piebald goat and the white goat; the twins asleep in her belly.

# Hang the Moon

When I was 13
it was Hammer Horror;
there was blood, it was springtide.

At 49 there was blood on blood.
It was Carrie and Psycho
and the Doctor said she was surprised I was upright.

Then the burning tongue
and sometimes I opened my mouth
and flames licked the sides of my face.

So, I shut my trap.
And for two years
ferrous sulphate did its quiet work.

And for two years
I didn't speak of it
and fire ate my words.

How tiresome anyway
to hear the dull weep of blood
as a woman empties out.

# The Menstruous Woman

...bees, it is a well-known fact, will forsake their hives
if touched by a menstruous woman;

PLINY THE ELDER: *The Natural History*

It is never elegant to speak of blood.
A female body, tricked and out of whack
adjusts to wearing kindly black
to shroud the purpling of her clothes,
as menstrual fluid falls from her
too pell-mell for any shop-bought rags.

Not everyone is bold enough
to turn their menses into art;
to scriven gore across primed cotton board.
Some zigzag a passage through this cursed spell
with all the euphemisms
their red aunt instilled in them.

They are unreliable; leave work early –
say, twenty years too soon.
They become *a woman of a certain age.*
Who needs the foul embarrassment
of ageing female bodies in a public place?
Who really wants to be deprived of all that honey?

# Brain Fog

shift of ragged lacework
over gospel facts –
    like the alphabet
    or the exact word to describe
        this ghost that's come in
        and is wearing my face.

\*

fallen map
    an oily smirch on the wall.

\*

that 'terrible fish'
at the brim of a pond
    cauldron of vinegar
    stirred up by a dirty oar.

# The Change

You sit inside yourself
and your body does its thing.
One minute it's a honeypot of oestrogen
the next, the head you had grown up with
is a crucible – and the words *flushes* and *flashes*
don't touch the sides of this urge
to run clear of this chassis.

The clothes in your wardrobe
carry a whisper of mutton
from a source buried deep inside language.
You smear Lady Danger on muttony chops
and everywhere advice on how to hide your arms –
heaven forfend you make a spectacle
of your collagen depletion.

Every night your hormones throw a party
you don't want to attend,
messing with the levels like a bad DJ.
You read that tinnitus is affected by oestrogen's jitterbug;
that not enough research has been done.
Your skin is a rubber doll plumped up with lava
that's stumbled into a cold store at 4am.

# 'Invidia' ('Envy')

Engraving by Zacharias Dolendo (1596-97)
after design by: Jacques de Gheyn (II)


You wake as Invidia again,
burning up, heart racing like a cooped mare.
It's 4am and the sun hauls you upright
with its accomplice the blackbird;
her showy bright song insisting itself
into the electric shell of your ear.

In the engraving you eat your own heart
but it's too flighty to catch
so, you burn a path through the house
charring the carpet in your wake.
You catch your naked reflection
and see a changeling, muscled and prunish.

You open the fridge and stand in its light
but there is nothing to sate
and when the door closes
your evil eye takes in a picture
of a woman dancing, drunk,
flying arms plump with collagen.

She wears your favourite dress. You hate her smile;
can't summon how.
Soon you are ripping her up,
forcing a fistful into your mouth.
The carton of soy milk bought to temper this heat
helps to drag her all down your maw.
You are otherwise unsure of its voodoo.

shortly after midnight,
the house,
caught the flicker of an ascending light

she had wrought with her tools

this influence,
worse than the fine dust.

# Tick-Tock

All your life you've been expecting her to come rapping at your door. *Let me in let me in*, she pushes at the tender fabric of the shelter you'd assembled with your bare hands.

Don't you remember how they warned you about the woods? The woods are a darkly place, where you'll meet your darkly self and further ghastly things. Why did you go, why did you take your pretty light there? Why did you wear the woebegone smock of the crone when you could have been spring-step in a bright yellow dress?

And now she's in your bath, skin draping from her bones. And now she's taking off her wedding-ring, sliding it onto your finger with a gob of her spit.

# Thirteen Million

It is estimated that there are around 13 million people who are currently peri or menopausal in the UK, which is equivalent to a third of the entire UK female population.

NHS ENGLAND, 2022

Right now, I am a list of symptoms so cliché,
it's as if I've peeled off my living skin
and laid down inside a chalked outline.

And on the pavement next to me
are other women pressed into self-same woman shape
stretched along the street, further than the eye.

We've put down whatever we were holding,
removed our faces with something astringent
and here we are.

Yet the doctors, for the most part, shake their heads.
They were not trained for this –
we are just too complex and occult in our workings.

We are clogging up the whole town now
and other towns for sure.
People climb through us on their way to everywhere.

Younger women avert their eyes;
startle home to their mirror's reassuring purr –
*Oh yes, you are still the fairest of them all.*

# This whole thing was nearly never a thing

That time you checked yourself from all seven sides in the mirror before you left the house. That other time you scoured off the lipstick that bled from your lips into your handbaggy face, applied unguents made from babies and never actually got round to leaving the house. The week you tried snake oil on your neck, in your salad, injected it into your joints. And remember that whole summer when you wore long sleeves in the greenhouse heat because you didn't recognise your arms? The time you became imaginary? When they scratched out your name and overwrote it with somebody shiny? And what about the time they applied PVA to your surface and tried to emulsion over it? And when they attempted to sever your tongue with crimping shears because you'd *had your time*? And do you remember that dimensionless afternoon in September when you first sat down to write this and deleted the words before you even hit *save*?

# 34 Symptoms of the Menopause

A woman somewhere is typing on the internet
   *my heart wakes me up like clockwork.*
Now, another woman –
   *my whole body feels like a bee box too small for the bees.*

At 3am, a woman Googles      *burning tongue*
      another woman searches
            *cortisol, dying ovaries, blood sugar,*
                  *light sensitivity, vampirism, migraine.*

On a message board a woman writes
      *Does anyone else...*
another woman is typing
      *...yes, I can't leave the house I'm stone tired,*
                  *my underwear is sack cloth.*

      A woman reads about rage
            feels parts of her
                  skitter under the wardrobe.
      *Everything in the pantry wants to hurt me;*
            *sugar is hex, coffee is bad abracadabra.*

A woman, unbidden, pictures the dress
she burnt with an iron when she was nineteen;
      *irredeemable* she writes.
            *I sobbed right there, in the bank.*

*Is it normal*, a woman asks the women
      *is it normal to stand in a line-up of yourself*
            *and not recognise you at all?*
*Is it normal to be scared of driving, the washing machine, scales?*

*Is it normal to wake up in a bread oven night after night;*
*to flush blood away like you have emergency stores;*
*for words to fall from your left hemisphere?*

And all the women on the internet
faces blazing in the blue light of their screens, say

*yes, this is normal*
*we are here*
*we can hear you now.*

## Votive

To hell with your womb, that wandering beast –
you'll make a wax votive of your body; the whole cursed caboodle.
Before it sets, place in a snip of your hair, a single fingernail
and throw in intangibles, like how skittishness grips you
or dread can seep through your bones on a bright August day.
There are no absolute words for these feelings;
mark them in abstract, in green ink if you like,
fold up the paper, press it into the tallow of your belly.

It can be troublesome to expel a body from plaster –
a swift blast of freezing should trick it away.
Be sure to destroy it, the mould, when you're done –
each woman should make her own figure from scratch.
Now carry your votive to the woods, the hills, the sea –
somewhere close, where nature is her truest self.
When you've offered it, do not think of your body once.
Let the sun ease it/ the trees work their healing/ the sea rush it on.

# 'The Spirit of the Storm'

Frederick Sandys' study for wood engraving, 1860

There comes a point in very woman's life
when she transmutes into *The Spirit of the Storm.*
Why not grow snakes for hair,
conjure rain and lightning from your artful hands?

You've earned this wrath, don't squander it
on slapdash chores and sundry empty tasks
in the hollow of your living room –
get out and find a fitting auditorium.

They've been opining it for years
it should come as no surprise
when venom spouts forth from your breasts.
Lo! you are supreme, the most debauched of all bad mothers!

# ACKNOWLEDGEMENTS

Acknowledgements are due to the editors of these publications in which some of these poems first appeared: *Axon: Creative Explorations* (Australia), *Hanging Loose* (US), *The High Window*, *spoKe* (US), *Poetry Scotland*, *New American Writing* (MadHat Press, US, 2023), *Dreaming Awake: New Contemporary Prose Poetry from the United States, Australia, and the United Kingdom* (MadHat Press, US, 2023), *Dancing About Architecture and Other Ekphrastic Maneuvers* (MadHat Press US, 2024), *Setu*, *Wunderkammer: New and Selected Poems* (MadHat Press, US, 2023).

I would like to thank Neil Astley and George Szirtes for their continuing support of my work. Without them, I would have been a person in a field saying poems at the chickens all these years. In praise too, of all the strong female energy which has surrounded me while making this book – including Deb Alma, Gill Connors, Lucy Farrant and the Tilted Women.

Thanks too, to Chloe Garner of Ledbury Poetry Festival for selecting me for the Versopolis European Poetry platform; translations of some of these poems have appeared in Croatian and Greek for Goran's Spring and Athens World Poetry Festival chapbook publications; in huge appreciation of festival organisers Marko Pogačar, Marija Dejanović and Thanos Gogos for all that they do. I would like to thank Cassandra Atherton and Marc Vincenz for their many encouragements, and to celebrate my workshop group who saw earlier drafts of some of these poems: Tiffany Atkinson, Jo Guthrie, Andrea Holland, Andrew McDonnell, Esther Morgan and Jos Smith. I extend my thanks to everybody who has ever bought any of my books, and to those wonderful people who have been there on social media for the whole journey of this particular book and enriched my research.

You know who you are! Big thanks are due to Clare Shaw for expertly showing me around Pendle. My thanks are due to Arts Council England for the financial support which enabled me to research and write this book. Finally, my thanks and always love to Martin Figura who has accompanied me on all of my research trips from Pendle to Salem and has been the first reader of these poems as soon as they've materialised.

# ABOUT THE COLLAGE / POEMS

This way of working always feels alchemic to me; the magical process of transformation and creation. When making collage from pre-existing materials, each thing that you use is already charged with its own power. It was important for me with these collages to keep the rough edges and show the materials I used. Having seen the very handmade poppets and such at the Museum of Witchcraft in Boscastle and the objects used in the Spellbound exhibition at the Ashmolean, I wanted to get a scratchy folk-art feel to these. Apart from the first collage (*from the slant of her tone*) which I wrote and then cut up, the words for the others are sliced from sources such as fairytale books, *The Arthur Mee Children's Encyclopaedia*, and vintage women's magazines. I also use postcards and photographs bought from fleamarkets and make prints from vintage rubber stamps, and these are all made on the broken backboards of old books. Some may see breaking up books as vandalism, but I only use foxed and damaged things. I like to think that I give them a new life and rescue them from the silverfish.

MIX
Paper | Supporting
responsible forestry
FSC® C007785